MW01106569

SPECIAL CANADIAN COMMUNITIES

Chinese in Canada

Heather C. Hudak

Weigl

CALGARY

Published by Weigl Educational Publishers Limited
6325-10 Street SE
Calgary, Alberta
Canada T2H 2Z9
Web site: www.weigl.ca

All of the Internet URLs given in the book were valid at the time of publication. However, due to the
dynamic nature of the Internet, some addresses may have changed, or sites may have ceased to exist
since publication. While the author and publisher regret any inconvenience this may cause readers,
no responsibility for any such changes can be accepted by either the author or the publisher.

Library and Archives Canada Cataloguing in Publication

Hudak, Heather C., 1975-
        The Chinese in Canada / Heather C. Hudak.

(Special Canadian communities)
Includes index.
ISBN 1-55388-101-X (bound).--ISBN 1-55388-114-1 (pbk.)

        1. Chinese Canadians--Juvenile literature. 2. Chinese--Canada--History--Juvenile literature.
I. Title. II. Series: Special Canadian communities (Calgary, Alta.)

FC106.C5H88 2004   j971'.004951   C2004-904781-7

Printed and bound in Canada
1 2 3 4 5 6 7 8 9 0   09 08 07 06 05 04

Photograph Credits
Every reasonable effort has been made to trace ownership and to obtain permission to reprint
copyright material. The publishers would be pleased to have any errors or omissions brought
to their attention so that they may be corrected in subsequent printings.

Cover: Chinese Canadians perform a traditional dance during a Chinese New Year parade.

Cover: Masterfile (Albert Normandin); **CORBIS/MAGMA:** page 18B (Josef Scaylea);
Corel Corporation: pages 3MT, 9B, 20, 23R; **Digital Stock Corporation:** page 23M; **Glenbow
Archives pa-3441-46:** page 11; **Masterfile:** page 17 (DK & Dennie Cody), 19 (Albert Normandin);
Photos.com: pages 1, 3T, 3MB, 3B, 4T, 4B, 6, 7, 8T, 8B, 9T, 10, 12T, 12B, 13, 14T, 14B, 15, 16T, 16B, 21,
22L, 22R, 23L; **Jim Steinhart:** page 18T.

Project Coordinator Heather C. Hudak   **Design** Warren Clark
Layout Kathryn Livingstone   **Substantive Editor** Janice L. Redlin
Copy Editor Frances Purslow   **Photo Research** Andrea Harvey   **Consultant** Bo Li

We acknowledge the financial support of the Government of Canada through the Book Publishing
Industry Development Program (BPIDP) for our publishing activities.

Contents

Coming to Canada

China is a country in East Asia. People born in China are Chinese. Since the mid-1800s, many people have moved to Canada from China. Chinese settlers first arrived in Canada during the 1858 **gold rush**. They hoped to find gold. The first Chinese settlers arrived in British Columbia. They lived along the Fraser River.

The Chinese settlers hoped to earn more money in Canada. Many of them worked as **labourers** in poor conditions. They worked in sawmills, coal mines, and on railways. These jobs were dangerous. Most Chinese settlers lived in British Columbia. Between 1880 and 1885, 15,000 Chinese men helped build the Canadian Pacific Railway through British Columbia's mountains.

Chinese Canadians practise the **culture** and **heritage** of their homeland. They learn the songs, language, celebrations, recipes, and legends of their **ancestors**. Chinese Canadians have helped create the culture and communities of Canada today.

The Chinese flag has a large star that represents the government.

The Great Wall of China is one of China's most popular tourist destinations.

China

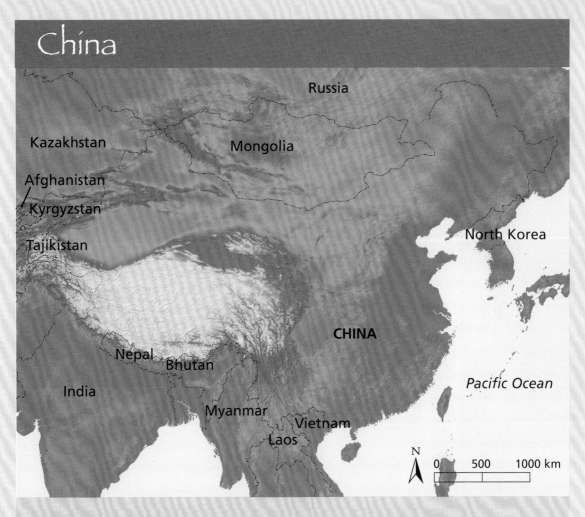

Russia

Kazakhstan

Mongolia

Afghanistan

Kyrgyzstan

North Korea

Tajikistan

CHINA

Nepal

Bhutan

Pacific Ocean

India

Myanmar

Vietnam

Laos

N

0   500   1000 km

Russia, Mongolia, and North Korea border China on the north. Kazakhstan, Afghanistan, Kyrgyzstan, and Tajikistan border China on the west. Laos, Nepal, Bhutan, India, Myanmar, and Vietnam are south of China. The Pacific Ocean is east of China.

Think About It

Can you find each of these countries on the map? What rivers, cities, and landmarks are nearby? What part of the world does your family come from? At the library, find a map of this country. Where is it located?

Chinese Communities

Some Chinese settlers came to Canada from the United States. They were looking for gold in California. They followed the gold rush north to British Columbia. They set up tents on the edge of a **ravine** in Victoria, British Columbia.

In 1959, Chinese settlers travelled by boat from Hong Kong to Canada. They arrived in British Columbia, where they built Chinatown communities. Chinese-owned businesses **thrived** in Chinatowns. Vancouver's Chinatown was a place where Chinese settlers could earn a living and be happy.

Many Chinese families moved east after the **Trans-Canada Highway** opened. They settled in cities across the country. Today, more than 50 percent of Chinese Canadians live in Toronto or Vancouver.

Chinatown is an area in a city where many Chinese people live, serve traditional food, and own businesses.

Chinatown Tales

"I came to Canada on a Japanese ship in 1912, when I was twenty years of age. There were about ninety people on board. I came to Canada primarily because my best friend talked me into it.

I disembarked at Victoria, B.C., where through one of my friends, I found work in a grocery store.

In China, boats called "junks" carry people and goods from one place to another.

After a while my godfather sent me transportation fare, so that I could move to the town where he lived and ran a restaurant with a friend. I worked in their restaurant until it closed, one and a half years later.

During those years most Chinese employers only hired their relatives or people who had the same surname. Even if you were hired by an employer to whom you were not related, as soon as he found a relative to take your place, you would immediately be fired. Thus, over the years, I moved around to many towns and cities, including Youngstown, Drumheller, Munson, Chinook, and Edmonton. I was very poor, but fortunately I met friendly, kind Chinese restaurant workers who would give me food to eat and a bed to sleep in. They always refused any payment in return."

From *The Chinese Experience In Canada: Life Stories From the Late 1800s to Today* by J. Brian Dawson and Nicholas Ting.

Think About It

Imagine it is the early 1900s. You have just arrived in Canada from China. Where would you live and work? Write a letter to family members in China. Tell them about your trip and life in Canada.

Celebrating Culture

Chinese settlers brought their cultural **traditions** to Canada. Many traditions include legends, songs, music, art, dance, food, and clothing. Many Chinese traditions are part of holiday celebrations. The Mid-Autumn Festival is an important part of Chinese culture. The festival takes place about the same time as Canada's Thanksgiving. During this festival, Chinese people celebrate the beauty of the Moon. They eat mooncakes, hang colourful **lanterns**, and host parades. Food, poetry, and music are part of the festival. The festival lasts at least 3 days. The Dragon Boat Festival is another important part of Chinese culture. This festival began in China more than 2,000 years ago. During this festival, people race through water in dragon-shaped boats. This festival is held at the beginning of June. One of their most important traditions is the Chinese New Year celebration.

Fresh Fish and Dragon Dances

Chinese New Year is a 15-day celebration that takes place between January and February. On New Year's Eve, Chinese families eat a large dinner, which includes fish. Each seafood dish is a symbol of luck, wealth, or happiness. Families play games until midnight, when there is a fireworks display.

The dragon is an important part of Chinese New Year's celebrations. The dragon is a symbol of strength, goodness, and good luck. During a parade, Chinese people dress like dragons and dance through the streets.

On New Year's Day, married couples give children red envelopes filled with money. This tradition is called the *Yashui Qian*. Then, families go door-to door greeting their neighbours.

The Chinese celebrate the Festival of Lanterns on the last day of the New Year. During this festival, they hang lanterns.

 The dragon appears in Chinese music, plays, art, and storytelling.

Think About It

What special holidays does your family celebrate? Think about these celebrations. Do any events or foods have special meaning?

Memorizing Mandarin

Many Chinese Canadians speak Chinese. Chinese is a tonal language. This means they speak in high and low tones to make words sound different. There are seven **dialects** of the Chinese language. Most Chinese people speak one of the Mandarin dialects. However, all Chinese people use the same writing system. Each syllable in the Chinese language has a character, or symbol. There are 3,000 to 4,000 common characters. Some dictionaries have more than 40,000 characters. Since 1919, the most common form of written Chinese is *baihua*. Baihua is a modern writing system. However, schools still teach some formal Chinese, which is called *wenyan*. *Pinyin* is used to write Mandarin using the English language alphabet.

For English speakers, Chinese is one of the most difficult languages to learn to speak, read, and write.

Learning the Language

For English speakers, the Chinese language is difficult to learn. Try saying some of the following pinyin words and phrases.

English	Pinyin
Hello	Ni Hao
Goodbye	Zai jian
Thank you	Xie-xie ni
Excuse me	Dui-bu-qi
Please help me.	Qing bang-zhu wo.
See you later.	Ming tian jian.

Chinese-Canadian children often take Chinese language classes in order to learn more about their culture.

Think About It

Try practising these Chinese words. How do they compare to the English language? Do you speak any other languages? Try writing these words in your language, too.

Painted Pottery and Wonderful Writing

There are many forms of Chinese art. Chinese Canadians often make this artwork to honour their heritage.

Shu fa is the Chinese word for calligraphy. Calligraphy is the art of painting characters. The painting is done with special brush strokes. The art of Chinese calligraphy is more than 4,000 years old. Artists use ink, paper, and a brush to write calligraphy.

Calligraphy means "beautiful writing."

Paper cutting is the art of using small scissors and a knife to make detailed paper patterns. Paper cuts have many uses. Chinese people give paper cuts as gifts, use them as decorations, and to make clothing patterns. Some paper cuts involve folding, cutting, and pasting many layers of paper.

Porcelain is also called "china." This is because the art of ceramics began in China more than 6,000 years ago.

Chinese people have made ceramics for more than 8,000 years. Ceramics is the art of making pottery and porcelain wares. Chinese people use special glazes and drawings to decorate ceramics. Some of the items they make include ceramic jars, cups, bowls, and figures.

Jikkan junishi is the Chinese zodiac. The zodiac is made up of twelve animal signs. Each sign represents a year. The cycle repeats every 12 years. Chinese people believe that the animal shapes the year's events. Some of the zodiac animals are the rat, rooster, monkey, and horse.

Traditional Clothing

Traditionally, Chinese people wore clothing made from silk, **brocade**, velvet, and satin. This clothing represented their culture. Many Chinese people still wear this clothing everyday or for special occasions.

Mao
hat

Yi fu
short
jacket

Embroidery
detailed
patterns

Ku
trousers

Qun
skirt

Think About It

What kinds of clothing do people from your culture and heritage wear? Do they wear it daily or only for special occasions?

In a Chinese opera, face-paint colours are used to show loyalty, bravery, wisdom, and humour.

Ancient Chinese religious and hunting rituals inspired traditional Chinese dances.

Dancing Days and Musical Notes

Music and dance are very important parts of Chinese culture. There are many Chinese dance and music groups in Canada. These groups perform at celebrations and festivals across the country.

There are two types of Chinese dance. They are folk and classical. Folk dances tell stories of love, war, farming, daily life, and celebrations. Dancers run and leap across the stage. Many classical dances are based on fairy tales and poetry. They use soft movements to tell the story. The Feather Ran Dance and Long Sleeve Dance are examples of classical Chinese dance. The dancers take small steps with their feet. They move their hands in special patterns.

The Lion Dance is one of the most common Chinese dances. Two or three people perform this dance holding a large lion head with a long cloth tail. Musicians follow the lion while playing a drum, **cymbals**, and a gong.

A common form of Chinese entertainment is the Chinese Peking opera. Peking opera combines music, dance, and martial arts. Performers wear colourful costumes.

Each year, Chinese Canadians take part in The Largest Lunar New Year Festival in Canada in Toronto, Ontario, and the Mid-Autumn Moon Festival in Vancouver. Dance and music groups perform at these events.

Poems of China

Chinese people learn special poems. Many poems were written during the Tang Dynasty (CE 618–907). Read the English and pinyin words of the Tang poem by Men Haoran below.

Zao Han You Huai

Mu luo yan nan du
Bei fang jiang shang han
Wo jia Xiang shui qu
Yao ge Chu yun duan
Xiang lei ke zhong jin
Gu fan tian ji kan
Mi jin yu you wen
Ping hai xi man man

Memories in Early Winter

South go the wild geese, for leaves are now falling,
And the water is cold with a wind from the north.
I remember my home; but the Xiang River's curves
Are walled by the clouds of this southern country.
I go forward. I weep till my tears are spent.
I see a sail in the far sky.
Where is the ferry? Will somebody tell me?
It's growing rough. It's growing dark.

Think About It

Think about the poems you know. Are they the same as the Chinese poem? Try writing a poem about early settlers, your community, or your heritage.

Delicious Dim Sum and Splendid Seafood

Chinese settlers brought many traditional recipes to Canada. They have been passed down to younger generations for hundreds of years. Vegetables add flavour and colour to a meal. Chinese people often use vegetables, such as turnip, radish, spring onions, and mushrooms, in their food. They also use **legumes**, such as black beans and bean sprouts, **tofu**, seafood, spices, and rice or noodles. Chinese meals are healthy and nutritious. They use a stir fry method to quickly cook foods. This keeps vitamins in the foods. Some common Chinese foods served in Canada are chow mein (fried meat and noodles), cha sui bao (pork buns), and jiaozi (filled dumplings).

Yum cha, or dim sum, is a special way to serve a meal. Dim sum means "touch the heart." Dim sum meals include bite-sized filled buns, noodles, steamed or fried dumplings, sweet pastries, vegetables, and meat. Chinese people serve about three to four of each food item per plate. This allows people to enjoy a large variety of foods at one meal.

Making Mooncakes

Follow the recipe to make traditional Chinese mooncakes. Mooncakes are special pastries Chinese people eat during the Mid-Autumn Festival.

Materials:

65 millilitres sugar
2 egg yolks
125 mL salted butter
250 mL jam
250 mL flour
large bowl
small bowl
wooden spoon
plastic wrap
baking brush

Preheat the oven to 190° Celsius .

In a large bowl, mix the sugar, butter, flour, and one egg yolk.

Roll the dough into a large ball. Wrap the ball in plastic wrap and place in the fridge for half an hour.

Remove the dough ball from the refrigerator and make many 3-centimetre dough balls from the chilled dough.

Use your thumb to make a small hole in the top of each small dough ball. Fill the hole with jam.

Beat the other egg yolk in a small bowl. Brush the top of each filled ball with the yolk.

With an adult's help, place the dough balls in the oven for about 20 minutes.

Serve hot, and enjoy.

Think About It

Think about the foods your family eats during holiday meals. Do any of these foods belong to a certain culture? With an adult's help, try making a special family recipe.

The *Chinese Workers Monument* in Toronto is dedicated to Chinese workers killed during the construction of the railway.

One Chinese worker died for every 1.6 kilometres (1 mile) of railway track laid in Canada.

Cultural Contributions

C hinese people have made many cultural contributions to Canada since first arriving in the 1800s. From the railway to war efforts, cultural centres to dance groups, Chinese culture is an important part of the Canadian identity.

In the late 1800s, many Chinese labourers died or were injured while working dangerous jobs. This included the work they did to help build the Canadian Pacific Railway. The railway united the ten provinces and became a symbol of Canada. Without Chinese workers, the railway could not have been built.

Hundreds of Chinese Canadians fought during World War II. They also raised $4 million for the war effort and bought $10 million in **Canadian Victory Bonds**. A memorial by artist Arthur Shu-Ren Cheng stands in Vancouver's Chinatown Memorial Square. The statue has a soldier on one side and a railway worker on the other side. It pays tribute to Chinese Canadian railway workers and soldiers.

Cultural Centres

There are many Chinese cultural centres across Canada. These centres bring together people of Chinese heritage. They also teach others about Chinese culture. Some centres offer language and dance classes. They also host Chinese festivals throughout the year.

Dance groups help keep the Chinese culture alive in Canada. They perform traditional dances for audiences across the country. Some combine jazz and ballet styles with Chinese dance. The Lorita Leung Dance Academy was formed in 1970. It was the first dance school of its kind in Canada. The Toronto Chinese Dance Academy formed in 1990. Chinese dance academies teach adults and children traditional Chinese dances, as well as modern dance.

Think About It

Think about your community. Are there any cultural centres and special groups? Which cultures do they represent? Do you belong to any special groups? Has any member of your family made a cultural contribution to Canada's heritage?

Many cities across Canada have Chinese New Year celebrations that include a parade, dancing, music, and food.

Further Research

How can I find more information about Chinese culture?

- Libraries have many interesting books about Chinese culture.

- The Internet offers some great Web sites dedicated to Chinese culture.

Where can I find a Web site to learn more about Chinese culture?

The Chinese Cultural Centre of Greater Vancouver
www.cccvan.com

The Chinese Settlers
http://collections.ic.gc.ca/pasttopresent/opportunity/chinese_settlers.html

Across the Generations: A History of the Chinese in Canada
http://collections.ic.gc.ca/generations

Colourful lanterns, sculptures, and dragon paintings are often included in Chinese architecture.

How can I find more Web sites about Chinese culture?

Using a search engine, such as yahoo.ca or google.ca, type in different search terms. Some terms you might try include "Chinese," "mooncakes," and "lion dance."

Design a Dragon

Materials

cardboard egg carton
yarn
paint
paintbrush
2 small bells
2 small pompoms
red felt
glue
2 plastic eyes
scissors

1. Use the scissors to cut apart six egg carton cups.

2. Paint the inside of one cup black. Paint the outside of all six cups in another colour. Use different colours to make special designs. Set the black cup aside. This will be the head.

3. Cut a small hole on each side of the remaining five cups.

4. Use one long piece of yarn to connect each egg cup. Cut the yarn so there is a small piece leftover on each end.

5. Tie a bell on each end of the string.

6. Glue the head cup on the top of one end.

7. Glue the eyes to the pompoms. Then glue the pompoms to the top of the head.

8. Cut a tongue out of the red felt. Then glue the tongue inside the mouth.

9. Enjoy playing with your Chinese dragon.

Think About It

Dragons are an important part of Chinese culture. Search the Internet to find other important symbols. What are some important symbols in your culture?

What Have You Learned?

1
Where is China?

2
When did Chinese settlers first arrive in Canada?

3
Where did many Chinese people settle?

4
What is the name of the most common Chinese language dialect?

5
How do Chinese people celebrate the New Year?

6	**7**	**8**	**9**	**10**
Name two Chinese art forms.	What animal is part of a well-known dance?	What is the name of a special Chinese meal?	Where is The Largest Lunar New Year Festival in Canada held?	Name two contributions Chinese people made to Canada.

Glossary

ancestors people from the past who are related to modern people

brocade heavy fabric with a raised design

Canadian Victory Bonds certificates sold by the Canadian government to help pay for the war

culture the customs, traditions, and values of a nation or people

cymbals a round metal musical instrument

dialects different forms of a language

gold rush a time when people from different countries move to a certain area in search of gold

heritage traditions passed down to younger generations

labourers people who use their body to do tiring work for money

lanterns a case, made of glass or paper, through which light can shine

legumes plants that grow in pods

ravine a deep, narrow valley

thrived did well; was successful

tofu cheeselike food made of soybean milk

traditions cultural rituals, customs, and practices

Trans-Canada Highway a highway that extends across Canada from Victoria, British Columbia, to St. John's, Newfoundland

Index